# BABE RUTH
## AND THE BASEBALL CURSE

by David A. Kelly

illustrated by Tim Jessell

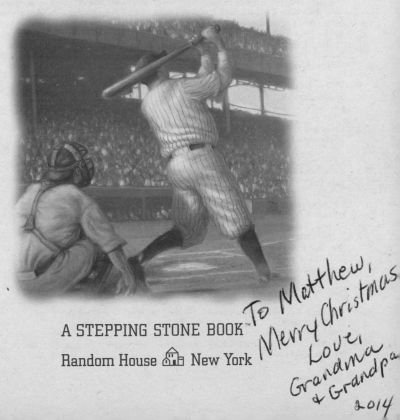

A STEPPING STONE BOOK™

Random House 🏠 New York

*To Matthew, Merry Christmas Love, Grandma & Grandpa 2014*

*This book is dedicated to the best team anyone could have—my wife, Alice; my sons, Steven and Scott; and my parents, Kevin and Nancy Kelly.*
*—D.A.K.*

*For Dad, who was stationed in Boston while serving in the navy and went to Fenway Park every chance he got.*
*—T.J.*

*Special thanks to Freddy Berowski of the National Baseball Hall of Fame in Cooperstown, New York.*

Visit us on the Web!
SteppingStonesBooks.com
randomhouse.com/kids

Educators and librarians, for a variety of teaching tools, visit us at
RHTeachersLibrarians.com

*Library of Congress Cataloging-in-Publication Data*
Kelly, David A.
Babe Ruth and the baseball curse / by David A. Kelly ; illustrated by Tim Jessell.
p. cm.
"A Stepping Stone Book."
ISBN 978-0-375-85603-7 (pbk.) — ISBN 978-0-375-95603-4 (lib. bdg.)
1. Ruth, Babe, 1895–1948—Juvenile literature. 2. Baseball players—
United States—Biography—Juvenile literature. 3. Boston Red Sox
(Baseball team)—History—Juvenile literature. 4. New York Yankees
(Baseball team)—History—Juvenile literature. 5. Baseball—History. I. Title.
GV865.R8K45 2009     796.357092—dc22     [B]     2008018004

Printed in the United States of America     11 10 9 8 7 6

# Contents

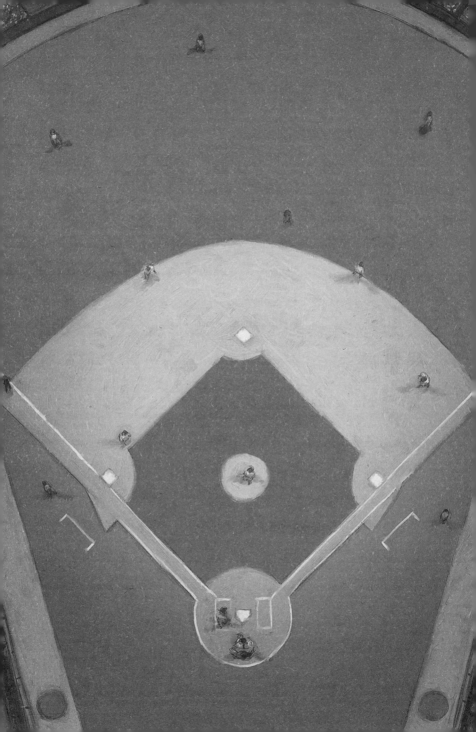

# Five Outs Away

October 16, 2003, was a chilly night at Yankee Stadium. But the Boston Red Sox fans there barely noticed the cold. Their team was close to beating the New York Yankees. If the Red Sox won, they would play in the World Series for the first time since 1986.

The Boston fans stomped their feet and cheered loudly. The Red Sox were ahead by three runs in the eighth inning. Only one more inning after this and they'd win.

Boston's ace pitcher, Pedro Martinez, was on the mound. He had pitched well, but it was late in the game. He had thrown a lot of pitches. His hands were cold.

Derek Jeter, a star hitter for the Yankees, waited for the next pitch. Pedro threw a fastball. Jeter smacked a double. Pedro was angry. He took his time before pitching again. The next batter hit a single and Jeter scored. One man was on base, but the Red Sox were still ahead by two runs.

TV cameras zoomed in on Pedro. He looked tired. He needed two outs to end the inning. Grady Little, the Red Sox manager, ambled to the mound. Should he take Pedro out of the game? A new pitcher would have more energy. A new pitcher might easily get the two outs. But Pedro was a star.

The crowd got quiet. Little talked to Pedro, then headed back to the dugout. He decided to let Pedro keep going. His decision would have big results—big, *bad* results for the Boston Red Sox.

Pedro glared at the next batter and adjusted his hat. He blew on his hands to warm them.

He threw the baseball. The batter swung and blasted a double.

From behind his glove, Pedro looked nervously at the next batter. He pitched again. *Pow!* Another double! Two Yankees scored! The game was tied, Red Sox 5–Yankees 5. Finally Grady Little pulled Pedro out of the game and replaced him with another pitcher. Two outs later, the inning was over.

To win, the Red Sox would have to

break the tie. But neither team scored in the ninth inning. The game went into extra innings. Nobody scored in the tenth inning.

The Red Sox didn't score in the beginning of the eleventh. It was the Yankees' turn to try to break the tie.

Aaron Boone was the first Yankee batter. Boone wasn't a star. Many Yankee fans didn't even know who he was.

Boone swung at the first pitch. *Bam!* He hit it hard. The ball soared over the third baseman's head.

Boston fans held their breath.

The ball kept going.

It flew past the left fielder.

It finally fell into the left-field seats. Aaron Boone had hit a "walk-off" home run—a home run that ended the game.

The Yankees won, 6 to 5! The Yankee fans exploded with happiness. Their team was going to the World Series!

Boston fans were stunned. How could they have lost? They had been ahead by three runs in the eighth inning. . . .

There would be no World Series championship for Boston this year. No World Series rings. No place to go but home. Once again, the Boston Red Sox had been hit with bad luck.

The Red Sox knew all about bad luck. They were famous for it. They'd had bad luck for over eighty years, ever since 1920. That's the year they sold Babe Ruth, one of the best players of all time. And who did the Red Sox sell Babe Ruth to? The team that would quickly become their fiercest rival— the New York Yankees!

With the Babe, the Yankees played in seven World Series.

Without the Babe, the Red Sox fell to the

bottom of the standings and struggled for years. They made it into the World Series only a few times. Each time they made it to the World Series or even got close, they suffered a heartbreaking loss.

Some fans thought the Red Sox were jinxed because of the sale. They thought the Red Sox were doomed to fail because of Babe Ruth and the baseball curse.

# Turning Trouble into Good Luck

Babe Ruth's life was full of good luck . . . and bad. When he was a kid, it was mostly bad luck.

Back then, he was called George Herman Ruth. His childhood was hard and his parents poor. Six of his seven brothers and sisters died as babies. His parents were too busy working to take care of him. That left Ruth plenty of time to get into trouble.

He got into so much trouble that when he was seven, his father sent him to St. Mary's Industrial School for Boys. St. Mary's was a school in Baltimore for boys who were orphans. It was also for boys whose parents didn't or couldn't take good care of them. Parents were allowed to visit their children one Sunday a month and on holidays. But during the twelve years that Ruth was at the school, his parents rarely showed up. He only went home a few times. He was very lonely.

At school Ruth found the strict routines hard. The people who worked at St. Mary's said he was "incorrigible." That meant he didn't behave well. He was a problem.

But being difficult probably helped Ruth. Boys who got into trouble had to see Brother Matthias. Brother Matthias was in

charge of discipline at the school. But he was also in charge of the school's baseball team. He saw something special in Ruth. He taught Ruth how to play baseball.

Brother Matthias was a tall, strong man. He could belt a baseball farther than Ruth ever thought possible. Ruth tried to be like him. He wanted to do everything that Brother Matthias did. He copied his walk. He copied his swing. Ruth learned quickly. By the time he was twelve, Ruth was playing with sixteen-year-old boys.

But even on the baseball team, Ruth got into trouble. One time, his big mouth got him into a fix that changed the rest of his life. As usual, Ruth was playing catcher for his team. The other team was beating them badly. They were getting lots of hits and scoring lots of runs.

Ruth's team switched pitchers, but it didn't help. Crouching behind the plate, Ruth finally couldn't take it anymore. He burst out laughing at his own pitcher!

Brother Matthias was not happy. He called a time-out and walked over to Ruth. Brother Matthias asked why he was laughing. Ruth told him he was laughing because the pitcher couldn't throw a ball that the other team couldn't hit.

Brother Matthias decided to teach Ruth a lesson. He told him to go out to the mound and pitch.

Ruth stopped laughing. He had never pitched in his life! There was no way he could pitch now.

Brother Matthias wouldn't listen. Since Ruth knew so much about pitching, he should show his team how it was done!

Ruth was ashamed. He took off his catcher's equipment. He borrowed a glove and walked to the mound. He didn't know where to start.

On the mound, he tried to figure out where to put his feet. He turned and pulled his large, strong body into position. Suddenly he felt comfortable. The pitching position felt right to him. Out of nowhere, he threw a blazing fast pitch. It seemed like the most natural thing in the world!

For the rest of his years at the school, Ruth was a pitcher. Then one day in February 1914, the owner of a minor league team came to the school. Jack Dunn needed a new player for his team, the Baltimore Orioles. He had heard about Ruth and wanted to watch him play.

Dunn was so impressed that he asked

Ruth to join the Baltimore Orioles. Ruth was just nineteen years old. He was amazed that anyone would ask him to play baseball for a living.

Then Dunn said that Ruth would earn $600 a year! Ruth's jaw dropped. Not only was he going to play baseball, but they were going to pay him for it! He couldn't believe his good luck. But since Ruth was young and still in school, Dunn had to sign paperwork to become Ruth's legal guardian. Newspapers in Baltimore called Ruth "Dunn's babe."

A few weeks later, Ruth left St. Mary's behind. He boarded a train to North Carolina for spring training with the Orioles. A few months later, Ruth was sold to the Boston Red Sox. In a very short time, George Herman Ruth had gone from being a troubled kid in school to being a major league pitcher for one of America's top teams.

Would bad luck follow him to the Red Sox? Or good luck? Or perhaps both?

# From Rookie to Star

When Ruth joined the Boston Red Sox, they were one of the best teams in the league.

They had won the very first World Series in 1903. In fact, the Red Sox were so good that they won five of the first fifteen World Series!

During that same time, the New York Yankees never even made it to the World

Series. They played very badly. Many seasons they finished in last place.

Ruth wasn't quite ready to play major league baseball. At first the Red Sox sent him to their minor league team in Providence, Rhode Island. In Providence, he helped make the team the best in the league. By the end of the season, Ruth had moved up to the Boston Red Sox and Fenway Park.

Fenway Park is the home of the Boston Red Sox. Today it is the oldest major league baseball stadium. The Red Sox have played there since 1912. It opened the same week that the famous ship the *Titanic* sunk.

When he first joined the team, his teammates went out of their way to tease Ruth because he was new. Sometimes they were even mean to him. They sawed his bats in two. Sometimes they wouldn't let him go near the batting cage. As a pitcher, he was supposed to pitch well, not bat well.

But Ruth pitched well for the Red Sox, and his teammates grew to like him. He pitched in four games in that first year and won two. It was a good start for a young pitcher.

After the season, Ruth married a waitress he met at a coffee shop in Boston. Her name was Helen Woodford. They bought a small farmhouse in Sudbury, Massachusetts, about thirty minutes west of Boston.

In 1915, Ruth's pitching was better than ever. He won eighteen games for the Red Sox and lost only eight. That's a very good record. He also hit four home runs that year. They were the first home runs of his major league career. Four might not sound like a lot, but the entire team only hit ten home runs that year! He helped the Red Sox make it to the World Series, where they won again.

Even though he was now a professional baseball player, Ruth never seemed to grow up. He even had a big smiley face like a baby's. Ruth's nickname was "the Bambino," which means "baby" in Italian.

Many times he acted like a kid. He liked pulling silly stunts, trying new things, and simply horsing around. Ruth was often more interested in having fun than in doing what he was supposed to do. Sometimes he wore the same underwear for days at a time. He just didn't feel like changing. He claimed to be able to burp louder than a tractor. He'd prove it to anyone who would listen.

Back in his first spring-training session with the Baltimore Orioles, Ruth had spent hours riding up and down in the elevator. He had never been in an elevator before. He loved the way it whooshed between floors.

At that time, elevators had people whose job was to run them. The elevator operators opened and closed the doors and pushed the buttons. After hours of riding the elevator, Ruth talked the operator into letting him handle the controls. Ruth gave the elevator operator most of his money to let him try.

But Ruth was so excited that he forgot to close the door of the elevator. He was still looking down the hallway when he pushed the UP button. *Whoosh!* The elevator started up with Ruth leaning halfway out. His friends yelled for him to watch out! Ruth stepped back just in time. He barely escaped a very bad accident.

But the team's manager found out. He

gave Ruth a terrific bawling out. Ruth felt ashamed. He had almost hurt himself while fooling around.

Ruth was so sad that his teammates took pity on him. His manager said that he was just like a "babe in the woods." That's another way of saying he was kind of innocent. From then on, the rest of his team just called him "Babe." It's a nickname he would have for the rest of his life.

Even though he was a "babe," Ruth was amazing on the field. He was a powerful pitcher. For example, in 1917, he won twenty-four games! He even pitched thirty-five complete games. That means that he pitched the whole nine innings, from start to end, by himself. That rarely happens today.

In the 1916 World Series, Babe Ruth pitched a fourteen-inning complete game.

It's a record that still stands. In one of the games in the 1918 World Series, Ruth didn't give up a single run to the other team. That's called a shutout.

Babe Ruth was one of the best pitchers in the world. His good luck at escaping a life of poverty had rubbed off on the Red Sox. Ruth helped them win three World Series— in 1915, 1916, and 1918.

For Babe Ruth and the Red Sox, 1918 was the high point. Ruth hit home runs. He pitched incredibly well. The Red Sox won the World Series again. It looked like nothing could stop them.

But the next year, 1919, something did. Maybe it was just fate. Maybe it was Babe Ruth's bad luck. Maybe it was the Red Sox's bad luck. Or maybe it was the start of the Curse of the Bambino.

# Babe Ruth, the Red Sox, and Trouble

The year 1919 was not a good one for the Boston Red Sox. In fact, for some Red Sox fans, 1919 was the beginning of the end.

It should have been a great year for the team. They had won the World Series in 1918. Babe Ruth was their star pitcher. Many people thought they would come back in October to win another World Series. But they didn't.

It started off badly for both the Red Sox

and Babe Ruth. In 1919, Ruth didn't show up for spring training with the rest of the team. He was holding out for more money.

Ruth had played so well in 1918 that he felt he should get a raise. He had made $7,000 in 1918. Ruth wanted $15,000 for one year or $30,000 for three years. But Harry Frazee, the new owner of the Red Sox, thought that was too much. World War I was going on and fewer people had paid to see the Red Sox that year. Frazee said he didn't have the money.

But Babe Ruth didn't give up. Late in March, Ruth and Frazee agreed on a new contract. It would pay Ruth $30,000 over three years. Ruth headed down to spring training.

Frazee and the Red Sox were getting a lot for their money. By 1919, Babe Ruth had decided he wanted to be a hitter instead of a pitcher. So instead of pitching thirty to forty games, Ruth pitched in only seventeen in 1919. But he played the outfield in over 110 games. That meant he had many more chances to bat—and many more chances to hit home runs!

Ruth's home runs were not enough for the team, though. By the middle of the season, the Red Sox had lost a lot of games. They weren't good enough to make it to the championship. There would be no World Series for the Red Sox that year. Their luck had run out.

But Babe Ruth was getting hot. He was hitting home runs. Lots of them.

Ruth used the same baseball bat in each game. It was made of dark ash wood. He wouldn't let anyone touch it, not even the batboys. Ruth carried it on and off the field himself.

One day, the bat cracked while Ruth was hitting. After the game, he sat down and tried to fix it himself. He used a small hammer, some tiny nails, and tape to hold the splintered bat together. It seemed to work.

However, a short time later, Ruth was using the bat when he was called out on a strike. Ruth thought it was a bad pitch, but the umpire said it was strike three. Ruth was out. He was furious at the umpire.

Ruth smashed the bat down on home plate!

CRACK! The bat splintered apart! His tiny nails and tape couldn't take the beating. It couldn't be fixed. Ruth stomped back to the dugout.

After Ruth calmed down, one of his

teammates asked him for the broken bat. Ruth said, "Take it." He never wanted to see the bat again. Later on, the teammate gave the bat to the National Baseball Hall of Fame in Cooperstown, New York. It's still there today.

Even without his favorite bat, Ruth kept belting the ball. Fans loved to watch him hit home runs, even if the Red Sox were losing. He made the game exciting. Ruth was thrilled with the attention. He knew that many of the fans were coming to see him.

Off the field, Ruth didn't always follow the rules. Sometimes he skipped Red Sox games to make extra money. People paid him to come to special events. But what really made his manager mad was when Ruth stayed out late after games and didn't show up on time the next day.

Red Sox owner Harry Frazee was also worried about Ruth. In 1919, he asked the Red Sox manager, Ed Barrow, to keep an eye on Ruth. He wanted to make sure that Ruth got to bed and had plenty of sleep. He didn't want Ruth staying out all night.

One time, after beating the Washington Senators, Ruth didn't come back to his hotel until after four in the morning! That day, the Red Sox lost. Barrow waited in the lobby of the hotel for Ruth to come back. But he didn't return. Finally Barrow asked a hotel employee to let him know when Ruth showed up.

At six o'clock in the morning, the hotel employee woke Barrow up. Ruth had just come in! Barrow got dressed and went to Ruth's room. He could hear Ruth talking to his teammate. He could see light coming from a crack at the bottom of the door. He knocked on Ruth's door. The voices stopped. The light clicked off.

Barrow opened the door and walked in.

Ruth was in bed. He had the covers pulled up to his chin, but he was awake.

Barrow went over and yanked the covers off the bed. Ruth was still completely dressed. He even had his shoes on!

The manager turned and walked away. He told Ruth to come see him at the ballpark later that day.

Babe Ruth was embarrassed that he had been caught breaking the rules. Still, he thought he should be able to do what he wanted. When he showed up for practice, he was ready for a fight.

In the locker room, Barrow was going over the rules. He was telling the players what time they needed to get to bed each night.

Babe Ruth exploded. They couldn't tell him what to do! If Barrow ever came into his hotel room again, he would punch him in the nose!

Everyone was silent. Nobody could believe that Ruth had yelled at the manager.

Barrow stared at Ruth. He told the players to get dressed and go out on the field. Everyone except Ruth. If Ruth wanted to fight, they would have it out now.

The players quickly left the clubhouse. The manager stayed. What would Ruth do?

Nobody knew.

Then suddenly, Ruth snuck out the door! He slipped away to the outfield and practiced catching balls with the rest of the team. He acted like nothing had happened.

Later on, the team came back into the clubhouse to get ready for the game. Ruth quietly walked over to the manager. He timidly asked if he was playing.

"No!" Barrow told Ruth to take off his uniform. Ruth was suspended!

Even without Ruth, the Red Sox won that day. That night, they took a train home to Boston. The team was happy, but Babe Ruth felt bad. He knew he had broken the rules. He was mad at himself for messing up. He decided to see if he could fix it.

He walked through the train and knocked on Ed Barrow's door. The manager invited Ruth inside.

Right away, Ruth said he was sorry. He told Barrow about his tough childhood and how much the Red Sox meant to him. He wanted to play again. He had an idea.

Ruth promised that if he went out at night, he would leave a note for Barrow. The note would tell Barrow what time Ruth got in.

Barrow wasn't sure it would work. He asked Ruth if he'd be honest about it. Ruth said yes. They shook hands on the deal. From then on, Ruth left notes for Barrow, telling him what time he got back. Barrow took him at his word and they never had another fight about it.

But that didn't mean that everything was fine. As the 1919 season went on, it was clear that most Red Sox fans were coming to see Babe Ruth. Ruth hit an astonishing twenty-nine home runs in 1919. It was a new record!

Since he was so popular, Ruth asked the owner of the Red Sox to double his salary. Ruth wanted $20,000 a year. But Frazee thought that was too much money. Ruth was a lot of trouble.

So Frazee found a solution. He sold Babe Ruth to the Yankees. The Yankees paid the Red Sox $100,000. That was more than any team had ever paid for a player. The Boston Red Sox owner was happy to see Ruth go.

"I think they are taking a gamble," Frazee said of the Yankees' decision to hire Babe Ruth.

At the time, many baseball experts felt it was a nice deal for Boston. Frazee had paid the Baltimore Orioles about $25,000 for

Babe Ruth. He sold him for $100,000. It was a good business decision.

But it was a bad baseball decision. Sure, Babe Ruth was trouble. But without Babe Ruth, the Boston Red Sox were *in* trouble. After selling Babe Ruth, the Red Sox did poorly. They didn't play in another World Series for twenty-seven years. They started to have bad luck all the time.

By selling Babe Ruth, the Boston Red Sox lost the heart and soul of their team. The Red Sox soon dropped to last place. And with Ruth, the Yankees soon made it to first place.

It was almost as if the Red Sox were cursed.

# The Yankees' Hero

For years, the New York Yankees were one of the worst teams in the league. They lost game after game. They didn't come close to winning a World Series.

But Babe Ruth turned their luck around. After he became a New York Yankee, things would never be the same.

Within a few years of buying Babe Ruth, the Yankees won the first of dozens of World Series. On the Yankees, Ruth hit even more home runs. In 1920, Ruth was one of the most famous people in America. He hit an amazing fifty-four home runs that year. That's twenty-five more than he had hit the year before. Fifty-four home runs was more than most *teams* had!

In 1920, the Yankees also became the first team to have more than a million people come to their home games. They soon built a large, new baseball stadium to hold all those fans. Yankee Stadium is known as "The House That Ruth Built" because so many people wanted to see Babe Ruth play.

Babe Ruth hit the ball hard. And he hit the ball far. Some of his home runs went 400 or 500 feet. Anyone hitting a baseball a long way was said to be "Babe Ruthing" it.

As a Yankee, Ruth broke lots of records. In 1927, he hit sixty home runs in a single season. That record wouldn't be broken for thirty-four years. By the time he retired from baseball in 1935, he had hit 714 home runs. It was a record that stood until 1974, when it was broken by Hank Aaron.

Of course, Babe Ruth still got into trouble on the Yankees. He still liked to stay out late. But he played well. Fans adored him. He was warm and charming, and he did funny things for the cameras. Children loved him, too. His favorite fans were children, and he often visited sick kids in the hospital.

But Babe Ruth was wild. He ate and drank too much and wore silly hats. He spent too much money. His midnight meals were larger than most people's dinners. Ruth thought nothing of eating six hot dogs and drinking six sodas for a snack.

He also had a terrible memory. He

couldn't remember names—even of his friends! He called teammates and other men "Doc" or "Kid." Older men were called "Pop." Older women were "Mom."

But none of that mattered when he was on the baseball diamond.

Babe Ruth led the Yankees to four World Series championships. They won seven American League pennants.

Babe Ruth played for the Yankees until 1934. In 1935, he played for the Boston Braves for a short time and then retired. In 1936, he was one of the first players elected into the Baseball Hall of Fame. Ruth died in 1948 but remains one of the most popular baseball players of all time.

Even after Ruth retired from baseball, the Yankees were the strongest team in the American League for many years. Since

Babe Ruth joined them in 1920, they've played in over thirty-five World Series. And they've won the World Series over twenty-five times!

But the Red Sox are a different story. After trading Babe Ruth, the Red Sox played so poorly that they made it to the World Series only four times in eighty years. And they lost every time!

The Red Sox didn't just lose. They lost in the most painful ways possible.

Boston would come very close to winning, but somehow they'd blow it. They lost each of those four World Series in the seventh (and final) games. With a few more runs or one more catch, they could have won.

There had to be a reason that the Red Sox were so unlucky.

# So Many Close Calls

Even though Babe Ruth never put a curse on the Red Sox, the Red Sox seemed cursed after he left for the Yankees.

The team played poorly and traded many of its best players. The Red Sox were no longer a great baseball team. The Yankees enjoyed World Series victory after victory, but the Red Sox seemed fated to lose.

Finally in 1946, after many years, the Red Sox made it back to the World Series.

It was the first time since 1918. They were playing the St. Louis Cardinals. Each team had won three games. The seventh game would decide the winner. With half an inning left to play, the score was tied, 3–3.

Then the Cardinals batter hit a double. Their man on first ran around the bases toward home plate. Boston's shortstop fired a relay throw home to get him out. It should

have been an easy play. But the throw was a second too late. The Cardinals scored a run and went on to win the game! If the ball had been thrown just a little faster, Boston might have been able to win.

Twenty years passed before they would get close again. In 1967, the Red Sox made it to the World Series. Again, they played the St. Louis Cardinals. It was a chance to make good on what they had lost in 1946, but for the second time, the Red Sox lost the World Series in seven games.

In 1975, the Red Sox had another chance at the World Series. This time they weren't playing the Cardinals. They played the Cincinnati Reds. After five games, the Reds were ahead by one game. Boston had to win the final two games to win the World Series.

Game six was so close it went into extra innings, with the score tied at 6–6. If the Reds won, it was over. If Boston won, they would play one more game.

Finally, in the bottom of the twelfth inning, Boston's catcher, Carlton Fisk, came up to bat. Fans loved him. He was a thrilling hitter to watch.

He let the first pitch go by. But not the second. The ball was low and difficult to hit. Fisk swung his hips and shoulders around fast. He hit the ball as hard as he could.

*Pow!*

The ball took off toward the left field corner of Boston's Fenway Park. Everyone watched it fly higher and higher. It would easily be a home run if it stayed straight. If the ball drifted to the left, it would go foul.

Boston fans held their breath.

As the ball flew toward left field, Fisk should have been running toward first. But he wasn't. Instead, he stared at the ball. He couldn't take his eyes off it.

Fisk started waving his arms to the right. It was as if he was trying to tell the ball where to go. If it stayed to the right of the foul pole, it would be a home run. He waved his arms some more.

Would it work? Could Carlton Fisk really control the baseball flying away from him?

Then something wonderful happened. High above the outfield, the ball bounced off the foul pole and over the left field wall.

It was a home run!

Fisk leapt for joy. A huge smile spread across his face.

The Red Sox had won the game! The series was tied! Fans thought it was the most exciting baseball game they had ever seen.

Maybe their luck was changing. Maybe they would win the seventh game—and the World Series—the next night.

But it didn't work out that way. The Cincinnati Reds won that game and the 1975 World Series. It was all over for Boston again.

Some fans started to think that the Boston Red Sox were cursed. Other teams, especially Boston's rivals, the New York Yankees, went to the World Series and won. Why couldn't Boston?

A few years later, in 1978, the Red Sox had another chance to break the curse. At the end of the season, they were tied for first place with the Yankees. To break the tie, there would have to be a one-game playoff at Fenway Park. The winner would go to the 1978 American League Championship Series.

From early on, it looked like the Red Sox would win. In the seventh inning, the Red Sox were ahead, 2–0. The Yankees were batting. Two Yankees had gotten on base in the seventh inning, though. That meant trouble for Boston.

Yankee shortstop Bucky Dent came to the plate. He was not a great hitter. In fact, he had hit only four home runs all season. Red Sox fans figured their pitcher would strike him out easily.

On the second pitch, Dent swung his bat hard. The ball bounced off his foot. Foul ball! Dent hopped around in pain. A doctor rushed out to check on Dent's foot. The minutes ticked by. The Red Sox pitcher stood on the mound, watching. He should have been making practice throws. But he just stood and watched.

Finally Bucky Dent was ready.

The batboy brought him a new bat. Dent stepped into the batter's box and waited for the pitch. The ball came sailing toward home plate. Dent saw that it was a good pitch.

He swung hard. *Pop!* He knocked the ball high into the air.

The ball blasted over the left field wall. Bucky Dent had hit a home run!

The two runners on base scored. Bucky Dent scored! The Yankees were ahead, 3–2. Boston was never able to catch up, and the Yankees won, 5–4.

It was a horrible loss. If the Red Sox had

scored just two more runs, they would have gone to the American League Championship Series.

But the pain of the 1978 loss would be nothing compared to what happened eight years later. The Red Sox would go to the World Series again in 1986. But their bad luck would follow them.

In 1986, the Red Sox faced the New York Mets in the World Series.

That year, the Mets were a powerful team. They won 108 games, which is very good. Many people thought the Mets would win the World Series, too.

But after five games, the Red Sox were ahead three wins to the Mets' two. Boston needed just one more win to capture the World Series.

The sixth game was close. With the

score tied, the game went into extra innings. Finally, in the tenth inning, Boston scored two runs. They were ahead!

The Mets had one last chance to bat. The Red Sox quickly got two outs. They were one out away from being the World Series champs! That would put their bad luck behind them forever.

The Mets needed three runs to take the lead. It seemed impossible for the Red Sox to lose.

It wasn't.

*Bang!* The Mets hit a single to left field.

*Bang!* The Mets hit a single to center field.

The Red Sox pitcher was nervous. He had to get that last out.

*Crack!* The next batter broke his bat but hit a single. One runner scored and the other moved to third base. Now the game was 5–4. The Mets were only behind by one run.

The Red Sox manager was nervous now. He put in a new pitcher, Bob Stanley.

The Mets batter, Mookie Wilson, soon had two strikes. One more strike and the Red Sox would win the World Series.

Stanley threw again. Something was wrong with the pitch!

Wilson jumped back. The pitch almost hit him!

The ball bounced off the catcher's glove and rolled away. It was a wild pitch! When a pitch misses the catcher's glove, runners are allowed to move up a base . . . if they can.

The Mets runner on third base saw his chance. He raced home while the Boston catcher was chasing the ball. The man on first ran to second. The Mets had tied the game, 5–5!

Mookie Wilson was still batting. He fouled off ball after ball. Finally Wilson saw a good pitch. He swung low and hard.

The ball skipped toward first base. The Red Sox first baseman, Bill Buckner, planted his feet wide apart and put his glove down to catch the ball. Buckner was normally a good fielder. It was an easy play.

Then the unbelievable happened.

The ball jumped. It rolled right under Bill Buckner's glove!

The Red Sox players in the dugout stood up and watched the ball roll into the outfield. It couldn't be true!

The Mets kept running. Wilson was safe at first. The runner on second base ran all the way home. He scored the winning run! The game was over. The Red Sox had lost the game.

Although the series wasn't over, it might as well have been. The Red Sox were not able to come back from their terrible loss and win the final game of the series. Once again, the Red Sox had lost the World Series.

Was the ghost of Babe Ruth playing tricks on the Red Sox? Did he give the ball a little nudge under Bill Buckner's glove? Or was it just bad luck?

# Spilled Blood

It took the Red Sox and their fans a long time to recover from the 1986 World Series loss to the Mets. They had come so close. And still they had blown it.

That's why the Red Sox playoff loss in 2003 against the Yankees was so painful. They had even been ahead! But then Pedro Martinez gave up those three runs and the Yankees tied the game. With a few more outs in October 2003, the Red Sox would have beaten the Yankees. They would have made it to the World Series.

When the Yankees won in the eleventh inning with a walk-off home run, it wasn't surprising. But it still hurt. Boston fans were so tired of being let down. They weren't looking forward to 2004.

But as the 2004 baseball season started, the Red Sox players felt good, even if their fans didn't. They came back from their winter break with a tough, scrappy attitude.

The 2004 Red Sox didn't look like other teams. In fact, many times they didn't even look like a team. Some players wore their Red Sox uniforms with their long red socks pulled up, while others wore regular white baseball pants. Some players had shiny new batting helmets, while others had ones scuffed and stained with black tar.

The manager didn't care about his players' hair, either. Long hair, short hair—it didn't matter. Catcher Jason Varitek had a stubby crew cut. Star outfielder Johnny Damon started the season with a full beard and brown hair down to his shoulders. Trot Nixon even sported a Mohawk for a short time.

For the Red Sox, the 2004 season wasn't going to be about clean uniforms or looking good. It was going to be about having fun and winning baseball games. It was going to be hard to come back from last year's heartbreaking loss to the Yankees. But the Red Sox were ready. They were gritty. They were hungry to win.

The Red Sox started out strong in 2004. But by the end of July, they weren't playing well enough to have a shot at the World Series.

They were making mistakes fielding balls. They fell eight games behind the Yankees. The Red Sox wouldn't make the playoffs unless something big happened.

In late July, they played the Yankees at Fenway. They lost the first game in the series and it looked like they were going to lose the second game. It seemed like the team just didn't have any spark. By the third inning, the Red Sox were behind, 3–0.

The Yankees' Alex Rodriguez, nicknamed A-Rod, came up to bat. The night before, A-Rod had driven in the winning run. So when the first pitch hit him on the elbow, A-Rod was mad. He thought that the pitcher had hit him on purpose.

A-Rod started saying angry things to the pitcher. Boston's catcher, Jason Varitek, quickly tried to calm A-Rod down. But

A-Rod was trying to pick a fight. "Come on," he taunted Varitek.

Varitek had had enough. Out of nowhere, he took his big leather catcher's mitt and stuffed it in A-Rod's face.

Both teams streamed onto the field. Players began fighting. The umpires and managers rushed over to stop it.

"You're out of the game!" yelled the umpire. Two Red Sox and two Yankees were kicked out!

After the game started again, everyone was fired up. Both teams got a lot of hits. In the bottom of the ninth inning, the Yankees were ahead, 10–8. The Red Sox scored one run, and they had one more trick up their sleeves. With a man on base, Bill Mueller hit a pitch clear into the Red Sox bull pen! It was a walk-off home run.

The fans screamed! Boston had come from behind to beat the Yankees! People thought it was the big break they needed. It sure helped the next night. Boston beat the Yankees again. Would it last?

No. Over the next few weeks, the Red Sox were still not winning enough. They were making too many errors.

To fix things, they made a surprising move. On July 30, they traded one of their most popular players, shortstop Nomar Garciaparra. Garciaparra was a good hitter, but his ankle had been hurting him all season. No one knew how much he would be able to play. So the Red Sox took a big chance and traded him. In return they got a new first baseman and a new shortstop. They also got speedy Dave Roberts from the Los Angeles Dodgers. Roberts was very fast at running the bases. It would end up being an important trade for Boston.

After a few weeks, the Red Sox started playing better. A lot better. The risky trade had made a difference. They were playing like winners. Three weeks later, they were only two games behind the Yankees! The Red Sox were hot.

Could they keep it going? Or would the curse still haunt them?

Maybe. But a strange event at a game in August may have changed everything.

On the last day of August, the Red Sox were playing the Anaheim Angels at Fenway Park. Boston's star hitter Manny Ramirez was up.

Ramirez was born in the Dominican Republic, but in 2004 he became an American citizen. Fans loved him for his powerful hitting. Sometimes fans got upset with him when he didn't run the bases fast enough or pay enough attention to the game. But he was always an interesting player to watch. One time when he was sliding into second base, he lost a diamond earring worth $15,000. It was never found.

On this day, Manny hit a foul ball like he had hundreds of other times. But this one was different.

A sixteen-year-old boy named Lee Gavin was in the stands. He was at Fenway for a birthday party with his friend. Gavin watched Ramirez hit the foul ball. It headed straight for his seat. Gavin stood up and reached out to catch the ball. It was his lucky day!

*Swish!*

The ball slid straight through his out-stretched hands! It smashed into his face!

*Thunk.* Blood splattered everywhere! The ball knocked out Gavin's two front teeth!

Medical workers quickly rushed him to the hospital. It wasn't that bad. Gavin only needed two stitches. Doctors were also able to put his teeth back in.

The doctors sent Gavin back to his house in nearby Sudbury, Massachusetts.

But Gavin's house wasn't just any house. It was special—at least for Red Sox fans.

That's because Gavin lived in Babe Ruth's old house! It was the same one where Ruth had lived when he played for the Boston Red Sox.

A couple days later, a Boston newspaper ran a story about Gavin and the ball. The writer wondered if the curse was lifted when Gavin was hit by the ball.

The same day, the New York Yankees lost to the Cleveland Indians, 22–0! It was the worst defeat ever for the Yankees. Was it a sign from the Babe?

In September, the Red Sox started catching up to the Yankees. They played great baseball.

At the end of September, they still had not caught the Yankees. But they had played well enough to make the playoffs as a "wild card" team. They beat the Anaheim Angels in three games to win the American League Division Series.

Now it would be the Boston Red Sox versus the New York Yankees in one of the most exciting American League Championship Series ever played.

# Three Games Down

To get into the 2004 World Series, the Red Sox would have to beat the Yankees.

Of course, fans in New York felt sure the Yankees would win. They always had. Since 1919, when the Red Sox sold Babe Ruth to the Yankees, the Yankees had won the World Series twenty-six times. The Red Sox had not won it once during that time. For New York fans, it wasn't hard to pick a winner.

Yet the Red Sox felt confident. One of Boston's best pitchers, Curt Schilling, was picked to pitch the first game. Schilling had already helped the Arizona Diamondbacks win a World Series in 2001, and many fans thought he was one of the best pitchers in baseball.

"I want to be part of a team that does something that has not been done in almost a century," Schilling said in an interview before the game. He was ready to win.

But after the start of the first game, Schilling was quiet. By the end of the third inning, the Yankees had nailed him for six runs. Something was wrong. Very wrong. Schilling was having trouble pushing off the pitcher's mound with his foot. He was taken out of the game after only three innings.

The Yankees jumped all over Boston's

pitching problems. They took control and won big.

Red Sox fans were stunned. Why had Curt Schilling looked so bad? Without Schilling, it would be almost impossible to win the series.

The next day, October 13, was another unlucky day for Boston. First the news came that Schilling would not make his next start. Then the Yankees scored three runs off Pedro Martinez in game two. The Red Sox got only one run the whole game.

They lost again.

Game three was even worse. No matter which pitcher the Red Sox used, the Yankees kept scoring runs. The game went on for four hours and twenty minutes. It was the longest nine-inning postseason game ever played.

The final score was 19–8. What a nightmare for Boston!

The Red Sox had lost the first three games in the best-of-seven series. They needed to win the next four games. But no baseball team had ever come back from losing the first three games in postseason play.

Once again, it looked like the Red Sox were going to miss out on the World Series. It was just another example of Boston's bad luck.

The funny thing was, no one told the Red Sox players that they should give up. Before the start of the next game, the team was happy. They thought they could win. Someone even put a message on the Red Sox clubhouse door that said, "WE CAN CHANGE HISTORY. BELIEVE IT."

Game four would tell. If the Yankees won, they'd go on to the World Series. The Red Sox would go home.

Although Boston led by one run in the sixth inning, the Yankees caught up. By the bottom of the ninth inning, the Yankees were ahead, 4–3. The owners of the Red Sox even started to write notes about what they were going to say to reporters to explain the loss.

Boston was up last. The Red Sox needed one run to tie the game and go into extra innings. Otherwise, it would all be over.

Mariano Rivera, the Yankees' best closing pitcher, was on the mound. He walked the first Boston batter. Boston put in Dave Roberts as a pinch runner. Roberts was fast. If anyone could steal a base or score a run, he could.

On the next pitch, Roberts exploded off the base in a wild try to steal second. Bill Mueller, the Red Sox batter, let the pitch fly by.

*Thunk.*

The catcher caught the ball. He rifled it toward second.

Roberts raced down the base path. He dove headfirst into second base, his arms outstretched.

He was safe! Roberts was one base closer to making it home. If a Boston batter could hit a single, speedy Roberts might be able to score from second base.

Rivera threw the next pitch. Mueller swung and connected with the ball. It was a clean hit to center field.

Dave Roberts ran as fast as he could. The ball was still in the outfield when he rounded third. He barreled toward home plate.

Bill Mueller stopped at first. But Dave Roberts flew across home plate. He scored! The game was tied at 4–4!

Since neither team had scored the go-ahead run, the game went into extra innings.

At 1:22 in the morning, the game was still tied. It was the bottom of the twelfth inning. Manny Ramirez had just singled, but the Red Sox needed a run.

David Ortiz came up to the plate. Ortiz was called "Big Papi" by his teammates. Ortiz, who was also born in the Dominican Republic, was large and powerful. And he was one of the happiest Red Sox players fans had ever seen.

Big Papi loved to play baseball and it showed. But he was also a great hitter.

When the Red Sox needed a run, they knew they could count on Big Papi.

Big Papi watched a few pitches go by. He was waiting for the right one.

He saw it. He swung with all his might. He drove the fastball high into the air. It flew far into the outfield and landed in the Yankees bull pen.

A walk-off home run for Big Papi! Ortiz circled the bases with a huge smile on his face. The entire Red Sox team was waiting for him. Ortiz jumped onto home plate. His teammates swarmed all over him, patting him on the back and head as he scored the winning run.

The Red Sox's World Series hopes were still alive!

They needed to win three more games against the Yankees to make it to the World

Series. But they didn't have to wait long for another chance. Game four had ended at close to 1:30 in the morning. The next game, game five, would start later that same day at Fenway.

Pedro Martinez pitched game five. He started off well and the Red Sox quickly scored a few runs. But by the bottom of the eighth, the Yankees were ahead by two runs. It didn't look good.

Again, "Big Papi" David Ortiz came to the rescue. In the bottom of the eighth, he led off with a home run to make it a 4–3 game. The Red Sox quickly got another run and tied the game!

It stayed tied for a long time. In the fourteenth inning, Big Papi stepped up to the plate again. Johnny Damon was on second. Manny Ramirez was on first. The two runners crouched down, ready to go. Damon would need to make it home in order to win the game.

Ortiz hoisted the wooden bat above his shoulders. He waited for the pitch.

Would he hit another walk-off home run? It seemed impossible.

*Swish. Tonk!* "Foul ball!"

*Swish. Tonk!* "Foul ball!"

*Swish. Tonk!* "Foul ball!"

Instead of hitting a home run, Ortiz fouled off ball after ball.

Two outs, two strikes. One missed pitch would end the inning and strand the winning run on base.

*Swish. Bang!*

On the tenth pitch, Ortiz spiked a hit into center field. Johnny Damon ran around third base, his long brown hair flying out from under his baseball cap. Could he make it home?

He did! Game over. The Red Sox won. Big Papi came to the rescue again!

# More Blood, Some Police, and a Winner

The Red Sox weren't home free yet. They still needed to win two games to beat the Yankees and get into the World Series. On top of that, the next two games were at Yankee Stadium, not Fenway Park. No major league team had ever won four games in a row in this situation. Even with those two great Boston wins, it seemed impossible.

A lot depended on Curt Schilling.

To pitch well, you need to push off from

the pitching rubber and land hard on your other foot. Schilling couldn't do that. The tendon in his ankle was loose. There was no easy or quick fix for it. It would take weeks to get better. But the Red Sox didn't have weeks.

Over the previous few days, the Red Sox team doctor had been working on a new way to keep Schilling's tendon from moving.

The doctor's idea had never been tried before. He went to a local medical school. He studied a leg that had been cut off a dead person. He opened it up to examine its muscles, tendons, and tissues. He decided his idea could work.

Before game five, the doctor gave Schilling medicine to numb his foot. The doctor stitched the skin around the tendon onto the deep tissue in Schilling's ankle.

Everyone hoped it would hold the tendon. If it did, Schilling might be able to pitch game six at Yankee Stadium.

Would Schilling be well enough to pitch?

Nobody knew. But when he walked to the mound for game six on Tuesday night, fans whispered to each other. Something was on his white sock, just above the edge of his sneaker.

Blood!

Drops of blood were leaking from Schilling's ankle where the doctor had stitched his tendon. The stitches stretched apart with each pitch. The circle of blood on the sock kept growing. But Schilling was pitching well.

Curt Schilling was giving new meaning to the name "Red Sox."

Even with his bleeding ankle, Schilling

wanted to get the Red Sox one game closer to a win.

Neither team scored at first. Finally the Red Sox got a run in the fourth inning. Then two more Red Sox made it on base. With two outs, Boston's Mark Bellhorn hit a ball toward the left field stands.

The ball went over the wall. But then it hit a fan and bounced back onto the field. It was still a home run! Three runs scored!

Or did they?

The left field umpire shocked everyone by saying it was not a home run! He said the ball was still in play because it had bounced off the wall. Boston would not get those three runs!

In seconds, the Red Sox manager was out on the field. He argued the call with the umpire. The game stopped. Everyone

watched the umpires come together to talk.

Finally the meeting broke up. They decided to overturn the left field umpire's call.

It *was* a home run! The Red Sox were ahead, 4–0!

Could the ghost of Babe Ruth be rooting for the Red Sox this time?

Schilling pitched well through seven bloody innings. The Yankees scored only one run.

Then in the eighth inning, things got strange. Bronson Arroyo had taken Schilling's place on the mound. Alex Rodriguez was batting for New York. Derek Jeter had just singled and was on first base.

A-Rod hit the ball back to the pitcher. Arroyo picked up the ball. He ran over to tag A-Rod out. Arroyo stretched out his glove with the ball in it to make the easy play.

Suddenly A-Rod swung his arm down and slapped Arroyo's arm. The ball came loose from Arroyo's glove! It fell onto the grass and rolled away!

A-Rod rounded first and ran to second. Derek Jeter scored. Boston fans were stunned. The rules say that a base runner cannot knock the ball out of a player's glove.

For the second time that night, the umpires held a meeting. A-Rod shuffled his feet on second base. The Boston players watched and waited. The umpire meeting broke up.

"Interference!" A-Rod was out! Jeter's run didn't count.

Now the Yankee fans were furious! They didn't want the umpires to change their calls. They threw cups and trash onto the field!

The Red Sox went back into the club-house for safety. Riot police with large shields streamed onto the field and stayed there for the rest of the inning. They knelt down along the sidelines in their blue uniforms and helmets. They thought the fans might be so angry they'd start fighting.

Finally the fans calmed down. The game went on and Boston won by two runs.

So the Yankees had won three games. And Boston had won three games. It would come down to the final game. The seventh game would decide who would go to the 2004 World Series.

From the start of the game, everything went well for the Red Sox. Big Papi hit a two-run homer in the first inning. In the second inning, Johnny Damon hit a grand slam to drive in four runs. The Red Sox were ahead, 6–0, in the second inning!

The Yankees scored a few times during the game, but by the bottom of the ninth inning, the Red Sox were up, 10–3. The Yankees needed seven runs to tie the game. It looked like the Red Sox had it in the bag. But fans remembered all the times they had lost in the past. No one was going to get too excited until the game was over.

The Yankees' leadoff batter hit a single. Then Boston got one out.

Two outs. Boston's pitcher walked a batter. Would the Yankees score?

Finally the Yankee batter hit a grounder past the pitcher to second base. The second baseman threw the ball to first, and just like that, the game was over. Boston had won the American League Championship Series!

The players leapt with joy! The Boston

Red Sox were going to the World Series!

They had beaten their biggest rival, the New York Yankees, in a series that even today seems unreal. They had lost the first three games. One was a 19–8 blowout. But the Red Sox still came back. They won four straight games against the New York Yankees, a team that had won more World Series than anyone.

So many times in the past when it looked like the Red Sox would win, something had gone wrong. But not in those last four games against the Yankees. Everything went the Red Sox's way.

Perhaps the ghost of Babe Ruth had decided to give them a break. Would 2004 be the year that Boston's bad luck ended?

# The End of the Curse?

The Red Sox had pulled off an amazing win against the Yankees. But they still had to win the World Series.

The Red Sox faced the St. Louis Cardinals. They had played the Cardinals in the World Series twice before—in 1946 and 1967. St. Louis had won both series in seven games.

But this was Boston's year.

The 2004 World Series began on October

23, 2004, in Boston. Both teams got a lot of hits. Halfway through the eighth inning, the score was tied, 9–9. But then Mark Bellhorn hit a home run to put Boston ahead, 11–9, and the Cardinals could not catch up. The Red Sox won the game!

Curt Schilling pitched game two at Fenway Park the following night. Again, blood soaked through his white sock, but he pitched well. The Red Sox scored in the first and led the game. Boston fans became a bit nervous when third baseman Bill Mueller made three errors. But unlike other years, the Red Sox got themselves out of the jam and won the game anyway. The final score was Boston 6, Cardinals 2.

Game three started two days later in St. Louis. Boston's ace, Pedro Martinez, was in top form. He pitched seven scoreless innings and gave up only three hits. The Red Sox won the game easily, 4–1.

Game four was the Cardinals' last chance to stop the Red Sox. A full moon was shining. Maybe it was an omen for Boston. The leadoff batter, Johnny Damon, smashed a home run into the bull pen in the first inning.

The hit took the fight out of the Cardinals. Boston scored two more runs later in the game while the Cardinals couldn't get even one. In fact, the Red Sox were never behind during any inning of all four World Series games.

But Red Sox fans wouldn't let themselves believe that their team was going to win. Even in the ninth inning, when the Cardinals were behind by three runs, many Red Sox fans held their breath. Their hearts had been broken too many times before by stunning, last-minute losses.

Not tonight. The Cardinals lost their fourth, and final, game to Boston by a score of 3–0. It had finally happened! The Red Sox had won the World Series!

Catcher Jason Varitek ran out to the pitcher's mound and jumped into pitcher Keith Foulke's arms. Players poured onto

the field. They quickly crowded around Varitek and rubbed his short, brushlike haircut in goofy celebration.

The stadium in St. Louis suddenly looked like it was in Boston. Fans threw their Red Sox caps up in the air. They held up signs that said, "THE CURSE IS REVERSED!"

Down on the field, Pedro Martinez hoisted the World Series trophy above his head like it was a crown. Base-stealing Dave Roberts leaned back and howled with delight.

"This is for anyone who ever played for the Red Sox, anyone who ever rooted for the Red Sox, anyone who has ever been to Fenway Park," said Theo Epstein, the Red Sox's general manager, in the locker room after the game. "This is bigger than the twenty-five players in this clubhouse. This is for all of Red Sox Nation past and present. I hope they're enjoying it as much as we are."

It was finally over. The 2004 Red Sox were the world champions! The last time Boston had won the World Series was eighty-six years earlier.

Just eleven days before, the Red Sox had been on the edge of another cursed loss. They were three games behind the Yankees in the playoffs. It seemed impossible for them to win four games in a row. No other baseball team had ever done it.

But the Red Sox did. Then they went on to win four straight games against the St. Louis Cardinals in the World Series.

"It's not the fact that we won the World Series, it's how we did it," said Curtis

Leskanic, one of Boston's pitchers. "We did it like no other team in the history of baseball."

After winning the World Series, the team flew back to Boston—at 3:30 in the morning. But they weren't alone. The thirty-two-pound World Series trophy was safely tucked into a seat beside pitcher Pedro Martinez. After the team got off the plane in Boston at 6:30 that morning, they boarded a bus to Fenway. Police officers on motorcycles zoomed ahead, clearing the road. Drivers pulled over to cheer, trucks blasted their horns in celebration, and people stood on the hoods of their cars to watch.

A few days later, the city of Boston held a victory parade for the Red Sox. Like everything else the Red Sox did that year, their victory parade was incredible.

Over 3.2 million Red Sox fans showed up. It was the biggest celebration in Boston's history. Fans hung out of windows. They spread out along sidewalks, bridges, roof-tops, trees, and any other place they could find. Everyone wanted to catch a glimpse of the world champions.

The party started at Fenway Park and snaked through Boston's streets.

Fans blew long red plastic horns that made loud buzzing sounds. They waved signs that read "THANK YOU!" and "ALL IS FORGIVEN." Boys and girls yelled out, "Go, Sox!" and the names of their favorite players. One man even painted a large blue and red "B" on his bald head!

"It started raining and it was cold and the people didn't even care," said Red Sox pitcher Derek Lowe. "They've waited a long time. You'll never see a parade like that with so many people, no matter what sport or what city."

The fans weren't the only ones having fun. Pitcher Pedro Martinez did a little dance. David Ortiz's big smile could be seen everywhere. Throughout the parade route, Ortiz kept raising both hands and pointing his index fingers at the fans. Their support had helped the team win.

The Boston Red Sox were back!

They were the world champions for the first time in eighty-six years.

From then on, baseball in Boston would still be magical, but it would never be cursed again.

# Author's Note

"I was a bad kid."

Those are the first words of Babe Ruth's autobiography. Ruth tells readers this not so that they will imitate him, but so that they can understand him. He wants us to know that people (like him) can learn from their mistakes and still do great things. When he was alone at school, shut off from his parents and misbehaving, it seemed almost impossible that he'd ever amount to anything.

Babe Ruth wasn't perfect—and he knew it. He could be loud and rude, and he broke the rules. But he never forgot where he came from and the people, like Brother Matthias, who helped him become a better person. The Babe always went out of his way to give back to children and fans.

It's interesting to consider what would have happened if Babe Ruth had not been sold to New York. Perhaps the Red Sox would have won more World Series. Perhaps the Yankees would not have become such a great team. But I'm sure that Babe Ruth would still have become a star.

# THE STORY BEHIND THE STORY

## BABE RUTH
### AND THE BASEBALL CURSE

### CATCH A RED SOX GAME IN FENWAY PARK!

**The Boston Americans.** The Red Sox were first known as the Boston Americans. They were one of the original members of the American League in 1901.

Charles Taylor, a Civil War veteran and owner of the *Boston Globe* newspaper, bought the team in 1904 as a gift for his son. He picked the name  Red Sox in 1907 and changed the uniform to include red stockings in 1908.

**Fenway Park** opened in 1912, in the Fenway section of Boston. It is the oldest major-league ballpark. It is also famous for its thirty-seven-foot-high left-field wall, called the Green Monster. It is the tallest left-field wall in the major leagues. The wall has a huge effect on games at Fenway, because it blocks a lot of flying baseballs.

**Wally**. The Red Sox's mascot is named Wally. He looks like a large green monster wearing the team uniform. Wally gets his name and looks from the left-field wall, the Green Monster.

# CATCH A YANKEES GAME IN YANKEE STADIUM!

**"The House That Ruth Built."**
When the Yankees bought Babe Ruth's contract in 1919, they didn't have their own home park. They played at the Polo Grounds, which was owned by their rivals, a baseball team called the New York Giants. After Babe Ruth made the Yankees more popular than the Giants, the Giants' owner kicked the Yankees out of the park. In 1923, Yankee Stadium opened.

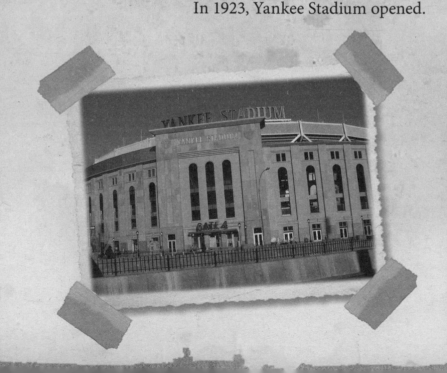

**Secret Room.** The original Yankee Stadium had a secret. There was a fifteen-foot-wide room hidden below second base! The stadium sometimes hosted boxing matches, and the room was used to store equipment needed for the sport. The Yankees removed the room in 1976.

**Pinstripes.** The Yankees uniforms are famous for the thin stripes on their pants and shirts. They first wore the pinstripes in 1912.

# Are you ready for more Yankees and Red Sox adventures?

## Catch the first two BALLPARK MYSTERIES®!

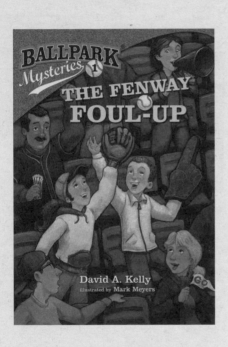

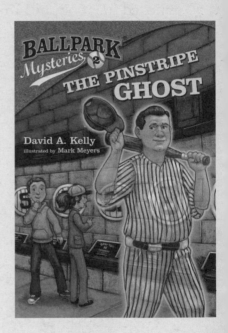

Batter up, crack the case, and learn amazing baseball facts with sleuths Mike and Kate!

# How many cases can you solve?

## Look for all the
## Ballpark Mysteries®!

# About the Author

Although David Kelly never had a chance to meet Babe Ruth, he did meet another home run king. One of his earliest baseball memories is of walking up to Hank Aaron in a restaurant and asking him for an autograph.

"Can't you see I'm eating my breakfast, kid?" Aaron said. "Come back later."

David did. Aaron, well fed and happy, gave him the autograph.

David has written for many newspapers and magazines, but *Babe Ruth and the Baseball Curse* is his first book for children. He lives fifteen minutes from Fenway Park in Newton, Massachusetts, with his wife, Alice; two sons, Steven and Scott; and a dog named Sam.